Hemispheric Dominance

The Indigo Child and Other Children

Table of Contents

Introduction

I want to thank you and congratulate you for downloading the book, *"Hemispheric Dominance: The Indigo Child and Other Children"*.

This book contains proven steps and strategies on how to determine hemispheric dominance, develop intelligence, and raise an Indigo child well. I wrote this book for a very personal reason. My son was behaving quite unusually. Every child around my place loved him. Once, he built a helicopter in our garden using bits of wood and paper found around the house. That was built inside a camping tent. Children played all together. Things inside the tent were moving thanks to the helicopter invention using the wind outside the tent. I understood pretty early that my son needed some special attention. His mother, my wife, died when he was 9 year old. When he reached 11, I realized that he needed something new and extravagantly different than a normal schooling system. I took him out of the system altogether and had him on a home schooling scheme. I registered him with the Open University. He was the youngest university student in the country so it was a challenge historically and academically for us both. His first university course was on robotics and programming. Soon, he would develop robots and alarm systems and would be programming all sorts of weird equipment around the house. He, as a joke or a hobby or fun, alarmed all of my rooms. For me, it was more like a nightmare. After a bit of research, I was introduced to the indigo child's world. That is where all started to make sense. You are now taken on from here for the special journey.

Thanks again for downloading this book, I hope you enjoy it!

Chapter 1. Profiling the Indigo Child: A Historical Background and a Checklist of Traits

Is your child 'different'? You may have an Indigo in your hands.

Indigo children are those with indigo auras. They are souls that are sent to Earth because they have a special mission to help out with the evolution of mankind and the planet itself. Many people nowadays are Indigos since we are fast approaching a turning point in history, and they are needed now more than ever.

There was a time when people didn't know what Indigos are until some investigated about them. These individuals noticed that there are some kids who have special traits, and more and more of them are turning up recently. Gordon-Michael Scallion was among the first few people who acknowledged their presence. He is a futurist who called them as "the Blue Children." Nancy Anne Tappe is a clairvoyant who can see auric fields – she discovered that babies born during the 80s and after tend to have indigo auras. The name caught on and these unique youngsters are labeled as 'Indigo children.'

Lee Carroll and Jan Tober wrote a book, "The Indigo Children: The New Kids Have Arrived." According to them, there were prophecies about people who will be born to change the world, and these are already coming into fruition. These authors studied Indigos a lot so they were able to provide numerous instructions about raising them well.

Jan Tober wrote another book with Doreen Virtue, "The Care and Feeding of Indigo Children." Wendy Chapman also published several articles about Indigos for parents and teachers. At present, there are many books, articles, websites and programs dedicated to Indigo children, and this book is just one of them.

It's good that you've decided to research on Indigos – the more you know, the better you can handle them. Raising Indigo children can be challenging because they are different from regular kids. However, it will prove to be rewarding since you are taking part in something that is important for the entire planet. Taking care of them means they take care of you too.

Characteristics of Indigo Children

You need not be clairvoyant to know if a child is an Indigo soul or not. These are some of their easily recognizable traits.

Warrior Spirits

Indigos are born to shake things up. Their mission is to break down structures and patterns that do not benefit humanity any longer. They have a keen sense of what is right and they will fight for it. Strong-willed and brave, they will enter many battles in their lifetime for the sake of mankind's overall progress.

Rebellious

Indigos will resist authority even at a young age. They are like this for a good reason – many dysfunctional systems are maintained because people have exerted unfair control over others. They will not obey authority figures and rules unless they are given good reasons to do so (being polite does not count for them). So, if they are being 'bratty', remember that this trait is part of why they are here.

System Breakers

Indigos are born with minds that are attuned to possibilities. Their creativity, above-average intelligence, and dissatisfaction with the way things are lead them to break systems and replace them with better ones. They will always prefer freedom over restriction, as this offers more opportunities for growth.

Leaders

Indigos are not followers; they are trailblazers and leaders. Do not expect them to be subservient or to follow a person or idea blindly. When they lead, they do not do so to gain power over others but to empower those around them.

Spiritual

Indigos are evolved souls, thus they are attuned to the spiritual realms. Many of them are psychic and interested in mysticism and spirituality. They have a talent for grasping deep spiritual insights easily. They may sometimes have extraordinary knowledge without learning about them from anyone – this may be the result of their extra-sensory perception or past life memories.

They Value Truth and Honesty

Since many lies have been disseminated on Earth, Indigos have a mission to eradicate falsehoods. Many Indigos are curious truth-seekers who do not hesitate to expose deceit when they encounter it. They have low tolerance for dishonesty because they are naturally honest themselves. Their perceptiveness makes them know whether they are being lied to or not, so you better not deceive them even if they're just kids!

Have a Sense of Purpose

Many people live life aimlessly; not so with Indigos. They know what they would dedicate their lives for. Because of this, they may not follow the path that you have intended for them. Take this to heart as early as now.

Knows About Own Uniqueness

The Indigo child will notice that not everybody is like him or her. People will often comment that he/she is kind of strange – this might get him/her teased and bullied. This does not make him/her want to conform though. It just strengthens his/her belief that diversity should be welcomed instead of ridiculed or feared. Many Indigos are proud of themselves and they encourage others to develop their self-esteem too.

Acknowledges Specialness

Indigos may behave like royalty because they have a high sense of self-worth. They know they are special and they expect that other people will realize it too. Their self-assurance comes from knowing that they have a right to be here, and other people's opinions of them are irrelevant to their duties. While other kids will change themselves to please their peers, Indigos usually have strong identities and will hold fast to their principles even under stress.

Smart and Tough Minded

It is said that Indigos have altered genes, which gives them advanced brainpower. IQs of Indigos are often above average, with some being geniuses. They easily find better ways of doing things, thus they are inventors and innovators. They are smart enough to perceive manipulations and tough enough to resist them. Because most of them are right-brain dominant, they grasp the bigger picture and ultimate outcomes of things.

Dislikes Superficiality

Indigos' brilliance and passion make them crave for meaning and despise superficiality. Their active minds are not easily satiated by hollow entertainment. They will often complain about some people's obsession over things that don't make sense. When they think that something is pointless, they will abandon it or change it to become more meaningful. They will avoid small talk as much as they could and go straight to the important topics.

Energetic

There are Indigos who have so much energy in them that weird things happen around them – electric appliances malfunction, watches stop, and so on. Some are even rumored to demonstrate supernatural abilities like telekinesis and levitation. More commonly, Indigos are highly spirited, active in a lot of pursuits, and may be restless.

Sensitive

Indigos' special energetic frequency makes them sensitive to emotions and vibrations. They may be easily affected by what others feel because they can feel them too. Their bodies may also be sensitive, thus they can have allergies, food intolerances, and the like. They can bond well with plants and animals because they can attune to their frequencies easily. They can also get along easily with people since they can see things from others' perspectives. This gives them an extraordinary understanding of people, and this contributes to the fulfillment of their missions.

May Sometimes Become Loners

Indigos may prefer to be alone so that they can work on what's important for them. Some can develop anti-social tendencies as well, especially when they are in an unsupportive environment. They may be mistaken with autism.

May Sometimes Be Troubled

It is hard to be an Indigo, thus some become depressed or even suicidal. They can become aggressive or withdrawn in response to their hardships. When they were not able to create strong identity, they can sometimes switch from having low self-esteem and a superiority complex. They may also resort to addictions in moments of weakness. Sometimes, Indigos can sense that they do not really belong on Earth, thus they ache to go back to where they came from.

Misunderstood

Indigos are often misunderstood. There are skeptics who say that Indigos are just people with ADHD or ADD and they should be treated as such. They claim that parents would rather believe that their troubled child is an Indigo to feel proud. Indigo or not, every child deserves love and care from their parents and will benefit from not being judged by people.

What to Do If You Have an Indigo Child

As mentioned, there are some people who are skeptical of Indigo children and explain their traits as ADHD or some other problem. The unfortunate thing about this is that they encourage the parents to give them ADHD medication to 'cure' their illness. Medications may indeed help 'normalize' a child's behavior, but they can dull the mind, suppress innate gifts, and cause unpleasant side effects.

This does not mean you should not listen to your doctor anymore. On the contrary, you should find a good doctor and cooperate with him/her in taking care of your child. Ask whether mind-altering medications are absolutely necessary or if there are alternatives. Observe the effects of medications on your child and determine whether it really helps him/her or not. Talk with your child to know what he/she needs – providing these may be enough to solve problems without resorting to drastic measures. Again, doctors are qualified caregivers – the trick is to find someone you can trust.

When it seems that you have an indigo, do your best to consider his/her unique traits and needs. Avoid trying to make the child become more 'normal' just so that it becomes easier to raise him/her. They normally have a duty to perform down here. Keep an eye on their attitude and habits to see if you can determine what that duty might be.

An indigo child is one of a kind, so he or she deserves extra care. This book will give you plenty of ideas on how to raise an Indigo well so he/she can reach his/her full potential. This is not about forcing your kid to fit in a mold that society approves. It will give you tips on what you could do and what you should avoid. It may not make your job easier but it will make sure that you will do a good job in taking care of your Indigo.

The main focus of this book is hemispheric dominance – the side of the brain that is more active. The brain is discussed so you will understand why your child is behaving the way he/she does. You will also learn how to nurture his/her traits while making up for weaknesses.

If you have a non-Indigo child, you can still use this book to raise him/her well. You will also read some pointers as to how to raise Indigos and non-Indigos in the same house harmoniously.

Hopefully this introduction made you understand what Indigos are. Let's continue learning more about them by discussing the brain hemispheres.

Chapter 2. Hemispheric Dominance: Deciphering the Left and Right Brain

The idea of hemispheric dominance resulted from studying different areas of the brain. Researchers observed patients who suffered damages to particular brain parts and noticed that they have particular effects on the mind and behavior. They also performed experiments and used scanning equipment (ex. PET and MRI) to know what goes on in the brain during certain situations and activities. All these research led to the conclusion that brain parts have specific functions, and these are usually common among people.

As you may have seen from pictures, the brain is divided into a left and right part. These parts are connected by the corpus callosum, which is a bundle of nerves in between them. Roger Wolcott Sperry and Michael Gazzaniga are researchers who studied split-brain patients with severed corpus callosums. They noticed some interesting things:

- Having a severed corpus callosum causes the right and left brain to act independently.
- Since the left brain is connected to the right side of the body and the right brain is connected to the left side of the body, a split-brain's one hand may perform an action that is unrelated to what the other is doing.
- When a split-brain patient is shown an image from the left eye, they can't verbally express what they have seen. The explanation behind this is that the visual information from the left eye goes to the right brain, which does not process verbal language.
- Holding an unknown object also produced similar results. When the item was placed in the right hand, the isolated left brain was able to describe and name it. However, when another item was placed in the right hand, the patient wasn't able to name this at all.
- Tactile tests revealed that the right brain is better with physical sensations than words. The split-brain patients were asked to reach for an item under the screen to match an image shown to them. They chose the correct object.
- Having a split brain also affects reasoning. A split-brain patient was shown a picture of a snowy field in one eye and a chicken in the other. Later on, the patient was asked to select words from a list that go with the picture. He chose a chicken foot to go with the chicken and a shovel for the snow, but when asked why, he said that the shovel is for cleaning the chicken's poop.

These findings made Sperry and Ganzzaniga conclude that the left and right hemispheres of the brain have specific functions. Later on, people got the idea that a person may use one half of the brain more than the other. This is where the theory of hemispheric dominance originated. Other people just expanded the idea.

Take note that many neuroscientists and other experts disagree with hemispheric dominance. They say that many activities that are ascribed to one half of the brain are really done by both of them. Even if these skeptics are right, you and your child can still benefit from strategies that help develop left and right brain potentials.

Most people say that Indigos are predominantly right-brained to balance the world's left-brain trend. Some assert that they are left-brained to represent the masculine energy of humanity. According to them, other special kids embody the feminine, right-brained aspect.

In chapter 5, you will learn what hemisphere is more active in your child. It is also possible that he/she is using both hemispheres in equal measure. Let's take a look at the roles of the brain hemispheres first.

The Roles of the Brain Hemispheres

These are the functions and characteristics that are commonly ascribed to the left and right brain:

Left-Brain Functions

- Causes awareness of time, details, order and sequence
- Monitors sequential and ongoing behaviours
- Assists in following a sequence or plot
- Processes information sequentially, one part at a time
- Gives the ability to recognize and imagine shapes as defined by the arrangement of parts
- Prefers objectivity over subjectivity
- Specializing in logic and analytical thinking
- Associated with math and scientific skills
- Concerned with precision
- Receives auditory information from environment
- Responsible for language, words, reading, writing, and speaking
- Gives verbal competence
- Helps remember names
- Establishes boundaries
- Helps in determining wrong from right
- Recognizes and upholds rules

- Follows deadlines
- Goal directed
- Involved with planning and strategy
- Oriented to reality and the past
- Values practicality and safety

Right-brain functions

- Deals with wholes
- Prioritizes the big picture over details
- Responsible for visual-motor (eye-hand) and visual-spatial (space-oriented) tasks
- Assists in the formation of mental images when reading or talking to others
- Linked to intuition and imagination
- Specializing in comprehending the bigger picture
- Considers information as wholes
- Processes information globally and from whole to parts
- Responsible for emotional responses
- Prefers novelty
- Gives the ability to tell whether someone is lying
- Enables the recognition of humour
- Prefers subjectivity over objectivity
- Associated with music, art, philosophy, and spirituality
- Assists in forming and maintaining social relationships
- Specializes in nonverbal functions
- Is linked to stories, images, symbols, and spatial relationships
- Involved with the recognition of drawings and patterns
- Helps remember faces
- Describes an object's function
- Helps with error detection
- Associated with greater environmental awareness
- Synthesizes details
- Helps in getting the point of something
- Considers possibilities
- Oriented to the future
- Encourages risk taking
- Uses random processing – works with information without order or priorities
- Involved with multitasking

Everyone uses both halves of the brain (even split-brain patients). The left and right hemispheres work together to handle each situation differently and to make up for what the other lacks. However, each person may seem to use a particular hemisphere more than the other. It is still best to develop both hemispheres, but learning may occur faster and more effortlessly when the preferred hemisphere is exercised.

Chapter 3. The Brain Quadrants: A Closer Look at Hemispheric Dominance

There is a model that supports hemispheric dominance but involves four quadrants of the brain – this is called the Whole Brain Model. William "Ned" Herrmann, a creativity researcher and founder of brain dominance technology created it.

The Whole Brain model is derived from Roger Sperry's Left/Right Brain theory and Paul McLean's Triune Brain model. The previous chapter dealt with the left and right brain so you will be familiar with what you'll read next. Here is a brief background of Paul McLean's Triune Brain model so you can understand Herrmann's model better.

The Triune Brain

Paul McLean is a neurologist who created the Triune Brain model. According to him, the brain is composed of three layers that developed during a particular period in evolution, with each new layer growing on top of an older one:

- The Reptilian Brain – the oldest part of the brain that is responsible for instinctual behaviours (ex. aggression and dominance) and automatic bodily functions like breathing, heartbeats, and digestion. It is said to be rigid, controlling, and ritualistic, thus it functions like a machine. According to theory, we share the same brain part with reptiles because we share a common ancestor with them.
- The Paleomammalian Brain – Also called as the limbic system, it is the part of the brain that we have in common with most mammals. This is associated with emotions and attention. This system gives the ability to label something as agreeable or disagreeable and the drive to seek pleasure and avoid pain.
- The Neomammalian Brain (cerebral neocortex) – This is the newest part of the brain found in primates and humans. Our brain's mass is composed of 2/3 neocortex, which is larger than most animals. This part gives us the capacity to think rationally and abstractly. The human brain hemispheres are composed mostly of this upper layer.

Herrmann's brain quadrants and their characteristics are as follows:

Left upper part (Cerebral): Logical/Analytical Mind

- Analytical

- Logical
- Mathematical
- Fact Based
- Technical
- Quantitative
- Linear thinker
- Oriented to the present
- Realistic
- Focused goals and outcomes
- Generalizes from specifics
- Argues based on facts
- Interested in goals and outcomes
- Rational
- Can be unemotional
- Gathers information
- Debates issues
- Evaluates and test ideas
- Formulates strategies
- Externally motivated

Strengths

- Checks facts
- Evaluates situations rationally
- Researches
- Good in creating reliable ideas and concepts

Weaknesses

- Can have a narrow focus
- Can miss the bigger picture or synergies
- Doesn't usually admit when they're wrong
- Can be a loner
- Not a good team player
- Prefers to work alone
- May have problems delegating tasks to others
- Prioritizes information over people

Preferences

- Clearly-stated information

- Conciseness
- Logical formats
- Certainty
- Accuracy
- Stimulating debates
- Critical analysis
- Research
- Readings

Left lower part (Limbic): Organized Mind

- Sequential
- Planner
- Organized
- Controlled
- Administrative
- Detail-Oriented
- Conservative
- Structured
- Diligent implementation
- Focuses on one thing at a time
- Tests and evaluates concepts
- Structures and sequences information and items
- Controlled expression
- Applies information and skills

Strengths

- Disciplined
- Controlled
- Can tolerate routine
- Good with details
- Logical
- Excellent with linear processing

Weaknesses

- Resists change
- Can be inflexible
- May be close minded

- May reject innovation
- Not good with creative tasks
- Uncomfortable in dynamic situations
- May not grasp the bigger picture

Preferences

- Detailed schedules and programs
- Punctuality
- Step by step processes/evaluations
- Explanations of the how's
- Structured methods and approaches
- Low risk scenarios
- Concrete examples

Right upper part (Cerebral): Creative Mind

- Imaginative
- Idealistic
- Intuitive
- Holistic
- Trailblazing
- Risk-taking
- Synthesizing
- Integrating
- Artistic
- Conceptual
- Inventing solutions
- Creating something new
- Visionary
- Optimistic
- Bringing change
- Future-oriented
- Perceiving the big picture
- Adventurous
- Entrepreneurial
- Considers the 'what-ifs'
- Forms systems
- Open-minded

- Intuitive problem solvers
- Intrinsically motivated

Strengths

- Ability to work with the big picture
- Creative
- Innovative
- Tolerance of uncertainty
- Good in making connections
- Intuition

Weaknesses

- May overlook details
- Dislikes repetitive tasks
- May rebel against rules
- Unable to maintain routines
- Can procrastinate
- Difficulty prioritizing

Preferences

- Overviews
- Conceptual frameworks
- Exploration
- Freedom
- Metaphors
- Analogies
- Visuals
- Initiatives
- Imagination
- Connections to other things
- Novelty
- Enjoyment

Right lower part (Limbic): Emotional Mind

- Free emotional expression
- Feeling-oriented
- Emotional

- Caring
- Interpersonal
- Networking
- Kinaesthetic
- Spiritual
- Expressive
- Musical
- Values relationships and communication
- Empathetic
- Nurturing
- Attuned to people
- Good with group dynamics
- Enjoys working with others
- Builds relationships
- Supports expression
- Team-oriented
- Likes emotional stimulation
- Makes connections
- Action-oriented

Strengths

- Focused on people
- Takes action
- Good with visuals
- Team player
- Excels in brainstorming
- Handles free-flowing tasks well
- Driven by values

Weaknesses

- May talk excessively
- May be too spontaneous and impulsive
- Acts without thinking
- Can get distracted easily
- Impatience with routine
- Uncomfortable with structured activities

Preferences

- Involvement with other people
- Personal stories
- Anecdotes
- Experiential activities
- Emotions
- Group activities
- Harmony

As you can see, this model is just a refined version of the Brain Hemisphere theory. You don't need to pinpoint the particular quadrant that is most active in your child, but you can use the information given above to help your child if he/she has certain tendencies.

Chapter 4 will summarize what you have learned so far so you won't have to memorize the lists. It also gives plenty of tips on how you could help your child with particular traits.

Chapter 4: Left vs. Right: Comparing the Two Hemispheres

The two hemispheres' traits and roles are products of the ways they process information:

Verbal vs. Non-verbal Processing

Since language is the expertise of the left brain, those with left-brain dominance will be good in expressing themselves through words. In comparison, right-brained children may struggle making themselves be understood by other people. They may prefer pointing to things or drawing them. When teaching right-brained children, use visual aids. Encourage them to make illustrations so they will learn the subject more quickly. Also, you may need to give them more time when writing something since they are not naturally good with words unlike the left-brained ones. Whenever I write a book, I need a professional editor and proofreader otherwise nobody would understand it. I'm really all over the place for the reader. I wrote and published my first book without any of these. The book got 1 star reviews just because of a logical flow not being there.

Sequential vs. Random Processing

The left hemisphere processes information in sequences. It relies on organization and order to make sense of things. Because of this, left brained children are list-makers. They like creating schedules and plans, and are usually disciplined enough to follow them. Their sequence-loving minds give them a high awareness of time, thus, some of them can tell how much time has passed without using timers or clocks.

Left-brained people's preference for order makes them stick to one thing before focusing on another. They plan ahead so that they have enough time to finish tasks. Disorganization bothers them so they avoid doing several things simultaneously. They also try to follow rules and meet goals as closely as possible. They are neat and organized with their activities and possessions. Although these traits are good, they can sometimes lead to trouble when flexibility is needed more than consistency. Messiness and unpredictability may overwhelm them as well.

Learning things in sequence is easier for the left-brained child. This includes memorization and spelling. Following instructions is natural too; you will notice that you will explain instructions to a right-brained child more than a left-brained one. As a plus, he/she may also excel in math and science.

In comparison, the right-brained student's approach is more randomized. He/she may be restless and switch from one task to another. It doesn't mean that he/she can't commit to something; a right-brainer can do what a left-brainer does just as effectively, but it's just that he/she likes to multitask. However, because the right-brain mind does not prioritize much, less important tasks may be attended first while more important ones remain unfinished. Schedules will also be restricting, and the child may forget about plans.

The right-brain's low awareness of time passing is a result of being engaged to the present moment. This could be labeled as having an 'in-time' mindset, where the focus is dedicated to what's currently happening, instead of having a 'through-time' mindset, which produces a detached view of time as a linear sequence. Being engaged to the moment means experiencing life more and being more available to other people. To make up for this approach's weaknesses, teach your child about why it's important to be punctual and to spend time wisely. Teach time management strategies. Give him/her a planner where he/she could write schedules and deadlines. Set alarms so he/she will remember what to do. It's likely that he/she is not checking what time it is already.

Teach also the value of paying attention to details. For example, show how it's important to read instructions and labels before using something. This is more important if the child is impulsive. For example, the wrong dosage of medications can cause him/her to feel ill. Not following test instructions can lead to failing the exam. Not reading the manual can cause equipment to malfunction.

Expect that the child may make careless mistakes. Encourage the child to go over his/her work before passing it. Let him/her use spelling and grammar checkers for his/her assignment. Go over his/her Math homework and check for errors. You must be consistent with this so that he/she will get used to being diligent.

Help a right-brained child learn sequences by appealing to the hemisphere's love for sensory information. Use colors, visuals, and sounds for learning. Use mnemonics/memory techniques.

Linear vs. Holistic Processing

The left brain works with information in a linear and sequential manner. It deals with parts, arranges them in a meaningful order, and draws logical conclusions from it. It is uncomfortable with the idea of creating something out of nothing. It prefers to work with pieces and put them together through practical methods.

The right brain works from the whole to its parts. Sometimes it ignores the details and focus on the entire thing or the 'point' of the idea. Because the right half of the brain works in non-linear ways, it can come up with an answer or a solution from out of the blue. Of course, it didn't do this magically; it's possible that several thought processes are involved, with some of them happening outside of the person's conscious awareness.

A right brain-dominant person is oriented to the whole, so he/she may find it difficult to follow a lecture unless he/she knows what the bigger picture is. This is why he/she will benefit from doing advance readings and knowing the background of a subject before learning it. When reading a book, it will help if he/she browses it first to get the main ideas. Encourage the child to get a copy of the course outline and let him/her refer to it whenever the details confuse him. If you could talk to the child's teacher, ask him/her to give your child an overview of the material before teaching it. Ask what the next lessons will be so you and your child could prepare for them.

On the other hand, a left brain-dominant individual will have no problems following lectures, but he/she may not care too much about what they mean. They might also find it difficult to read between the lines. To prevent missing the big picture, help the child connect details to the overall purpose of the lessons. Make him/her think about why the subject is important and how he/she can apply the information.

Symbolic Vs. Concrete Processing

The left brain is good with symbols. This means that left-brained pupils can excel in the maths, sciences, linguistics, and other fields that involve abstract concepts. They are contented with intellectually created ideas, and they are not concerned about working with intangible things.

Right-brain students prefer the opposite. They are more comfortable dealing with concrete objects and dislike learning something they can't interact with. Thus, hands-on activities are very popular with them. They may have trouble learning how to read with phonics, or simply sounding the words. They would benefit more if they observe the word being used in context. They want to see formulas working in real life. Teaching these right-brain kids will be easier if you use a lot of examples to explain a concept.

Logical vs. Intuitive Processing

The left brain is logical while the right brain is intuitive. When the child is left-brain dominant, he/she will process information using logic. He/she will prefer science and math because they involve logical methods. His/her decisions will be based on facts rather than feelings. Because of their traits, they can analyze something well and carry out procedures carefully.

A right-brain dominant child will be more intuitive. He/she may dislike subjects that require exact answers and prescribed solutions. He/she may even seem to be psychic as he/she may arrive at the correct answer without going through the expected steps of solving the problem. When studying, they may go straight to the result and work their way backwards. They may choose options based on hunches and how they feel about them. Their mind will zone in to the meaning and coherence of something so they don't need to bother with the details.

Reality-Oriented vs. Fantasy-Oriented Processing

The left brain deals with reality while its right counterpart deals with fantasies. Thus, left-brainers tend to cope better when their environment or situation changes. Since right-brainers are more in tune with their own fantasies, they may find it hard to adjust when the external circumstances become altered. To maintain a sense of stability, they may try to bring back how things used to be instead of changing themselves to suit the new scenario.

In relation to this, left-brained people are rule followers, while right-brained ones are rule breakers. Lefties desire order so much that they will make up rules if nobody has set them yet. Since they are attuned to how things work in reality, they know the causes and consequences of things. This makes them more responsible than their right-brained peers.

Right-brained people focus more on their inner worlds, so they don't give much importance to the rules and conventions of society. They may have low awareness of what's going on around them. They are not conscious of time passing, so they may spend too much time on something they enjoy or forget about deadlines. They will benefit from constant feedback so that they will not skip their obligations. However, despite being seemingly irresponsible, they tend to be more creative. If you want someone to think outside of the box, you can count on a right brainer to do it wonderfully.

As you may have observed from the descriptions, left brainers are more suited for traditional education than right brainers. This doesn't mean that right brainers are at a disadvantage. It only means that they need to make some adjustments so that they would excel in academics too. Consider home-schooling, tutoring, or enrolling him/her to a non-traditional school if he/she does not perform well in a traditional school.

On the other hand, left-brained students must not be overly confident, since being educated does not mean memorization and computations alone. They need to develop their right-brain capacities of intuition, empathy, and creativity to make the most of their schooling. Immerse a left-brain child in real life experiences and help him/her acquire a bigger perspective.

Now that you know about brain hemispheres and have ideas on how to develop each, the next chapter will teach you how to determine your child's hemispheric dominance.

Chapter 5. Left or Right: Determining Hemispheric Dominance

What hemisphere is more dominant in your child? You may already have ideas after reading the previous chapters, but for the sake of clarity, here are some specific traits to look for.

Left Brain Dominance Traits

- Can correctly guess how much time has passed without looking at a watch, but still likes wearing one
- Prefers learning something new by following a listed sequence rather than watching a demonstration
- Reads captions before looking at pictures
- Prefers algebra over geometry
- Likes completing one task before going to the next
- Responds more to what was said than how it is said
- Punctual
- Likes following schedules
- Interested in the details
- Processes information in a linear and sequential manner
- Responds to logic
- Planner
- Uses few gestures when speaking
- Benefits more from formal study designs
- Likes to have bright lights in the classroom
- Prefers objective test questions (multiple choices, matching, true/false)
- Carefully weighs options before deciding
- Recounts the details before telling a conclusion
- Organizes his/her things often
- Dislikes taking risks
- Doesn't change methods if they work
- Concentrates on a task until it's complete before working on another
- Carefully reads manual before using an item
- Thinks in words
- Thinks before speaking

- Can think better when sitting down
- Reads a magazine from page one and flips through the pages sequentially
- Saves money rather than spends impulsively
- Takes exact measurements rather than making estimates
- Likes using letters, words and mathematical symbols rather than pictures
- Thinks from part to whole
- Makes conclusions logically
- Analyzes what will happen next
- Does things step by step
- Follows rules and instructions
- Bases ideas on reality rather than fantasy
- Finds the best solution or the most correct answer
- Critical thinker
- Questions new ideas
- Disciplined
- Have no problems following other people's plans
- Doesn't have much ideas in a new situation
- Accomplishes important tasks first if they are important
- Likes an orderly and consistent life
- Knows that he/she is right because of facts and evidences
- Spreads work over his/her available time
- Manages time well
- Has consistency
- Has a stable personality
- Wants to be told what to do with a new task

Right Brain Dominance Traits

- Have hunches often
- Senses what will happen next
- Tries to find different answers to problems
- Knows right answer but not sure how he/she got it
- Processes information based on whether it feels right or not
- Follows intuitions
- Likes geometry over algebra
- Understands people even if they are talking in a different language
- Better in remembering faces than names
- Use hands a lot when talking

- Responds more to how a thing is said rather than the words
- Not so punctual
- Doesn't think about the time much
- Have problems sticking to schedules
- Does work at the last minute
- Procrastinates and crams often
- Delays doing hard tasks even if they are important
- Doesn't need a watch (but would benefit from one)
- Processes information intuitively
- Responds to feelings
- Acts according to how he/she feels
- Impulsive
- Risk-taker
- Creative
- Looks for ways to do things differently
- Have a lot of ideas in new situations
- Can focus more when there is music or sound playing in the background
- Goes with gut feelings when deciding
- Tells the main idea before filling the details
- Prefers dealing with generalities
- May be overwhelmed with detail
- Wants to know the point of things
- Can be disorganized
- Keeps things in convenient places
- Multitasks
- May jump from one activity to another without finishing
- Immediately tries using an item and reads manual only when needed
- Collects items that he/she may need someday
- Says what's on his/her mind without mincing words
- Thinks better when moving about or lying down
- Moves around while studying
- Prefers subjective test questions (essays, discussions)
- Opens a magazine and reads randomly
- Spends money impulsively
- Makes estimations
- Focuses less on rules and instructions
- Thoughts are illustrations rather than words

- Finds it easier to process tangible things (those that can be experienced by the senses)
- Daydreams a lot
- More open-minded
- Agrees readily to new ideas
- Prefers own plans
- Wants to find own way of doing a new activity
- Wants variety in life
- Insists on being right even without good reasons to back it up
- Very flexible
- Sometimes unpredictable

You can tell whether your child's teacher is a left-brainer or a right-brainer.

Left-Brained Teacher

- Prefers lectures and discussions
- Gives lessons according to an outline
- Prepares schedules and imposes it strictly
- Give problems that are solved individually
- Give students a lot of research work
- Frequently assigns writing tasks
- Insists students to maintain silence
- Sees to it that the students' desks are lined up
- Classroom is orderly, with things located in their proper places

Right-Brained Teacher

- Gives hands-on activities more than lectures
- Incorporates art and music to lessons
- Provides a lot of visuals, drawings, and graphs
- Makes the students work with manipulatives
- Targets the multiple intelligences
- Assigns group projects more than individual tasks
- Likes an active class
- Is not bothered by noise
- Classroom may be messy
- Seating arrangements may change a lot

How about you, are you left-brained or right-brained? One brain hemisphere is not better than the other, so you don't have to change your hemispheric dominance to make you a better parent for an Indigo. Just consider how your brain dominance may be affecting your child – for example, is your heightened time awareness causing you to be too strict with schedules? Is your disregard for organization confusing a left-brain child? Make some compromises and adjustments when necessary, but you don't have to overdo it. After all, being comfortable with who you are will help your child do the same.

Symptoms of Hemispheric Weakness

Just as a child may have a stronger brain hemisphere, he or she may also have a weak one.

Weak Left Brain Symptoms

- Difficulty reading
- Problems with fine motor skills
- Can't spell well
- Can't recognize letters
- Can't process sounds well
- Difficulty processing sounds
- Can't express self verbally
- Delayed speech
- Avoids academic tasks
- Misses details
- Constant errors in Math
- Lack of self esteem
- Lack of motivation
- Weak immune system

Weak Right Brain

- Hyperactivity
- Poorly developed gross motor skills
- Awkwardness
- Clumsiness
- Poor attention
- Can't focus well
- Impulsivity
- Inability to control emotions
- Difficulty expressing self non-verbally
- Can't comprehend no-verbal signals
- Inappropriate behaviour

- Low reading comprehension
- Obsessive
- Repeats behaviours unnecessarily
- Gets sick often
- lack of interest in sports
- Misses the big picture
- Doesn't respect other people's space
- Anxious
- Doesn't make eye contact
- Allergies
- Hyperactive immune system
- Immaturity
- Odd posture
- Moves strangely
- Consistently walks on toes
- Difficulty in learning tasks that require bodily movement
- Poor coordination
- Low muscle tone
- Lack of interest in sports
- Doesn't perform well in sports and physical activities

Weakness in one hemisphere may not be a cause of concern unless it causes problems. Seek help if you notice worrisome symptoms such as poorly developed gross motor skills, delayed speech, etc. Have your child tested for physical and psychological impediments. Getting checkups and the right treatments may help eliminate the bothersome symptoms.

After learning all about the left and right brain, it is now time to know how to make the most out of each hemisphere. Chapter 6 tackles teaching strategies that are appropriate to left and right brain learners. Keep in mind that the things you will read are only suggestions and not something you should strictly adhere to. Try different approaches and see what works for your child.

Chapter 6. Left Brain and Right Brain Learning: Hemispheric Dominance-Based Teaching Strategies

Educators have come up with several teaching strategies that are appropriate for left and right brain learners. If you are a teacher or a parent who tutors your child, consider doing the following for your left or right-brain dominant child.

Left Brain Strategies

- Have a brightly lit place
- Adopt formal approaches
- Use traditional teaching styles
- Provide a quiet environment
- Keep things orderly
- Arrange seats into aligned and evenly spaced rows
- Give structure
- Set schedules and deadlines
- State clear directions
- Provide plenty of opportunities for students to work by themselves
- Allow the child to solve a problem by breaking it down into parts and solving it step-by-step
- Solve problems the traditional way
- Provide verbal and written activities
- Build vocabulary
- Give crossword puzzles and other word games
- Hold spelling contests
- Give topics to research about
- Allow the child to read a lot
- Practice handwriting
- Teach how to read through phonics
- Make the child learn with auditory associations
- Make him/her listen to the lesson
- Discuss details
- Study facts

- Use critical thinking and logic
- Hold debates
- Do scientific experiments
- Answer math problems
- Teach math by explaining the rules and demonstrating how problems are solved
- Provide general equations with sample problems
- Solve puzzles
- Study history
- Play strategy games like chess
- Create something while following instructions
- Make them write for the school paper
- Discuss abstract concepts
- Give problem based activities
- Play strategy games
- Explain how you arrived at conclusions and solutions

Balancing a Left Brain Dominance

- Get to the why's of something (left brain dominant people are usually content without knowing the overall purpose and meanings of things)
- Help with determining the main ideas
- Teach the child how to be more flexible because left-brainers may get stuck with routines and processes
- Encourage the child to be more creative and explore different possibilities
- Help the child learn how to interpret non-verbal body language
- Synthesize details and explain how they connect with each other
- Provide a summary of the details that were discussed
- Make the child summarize the lesson in his/her own words
- Discuss a topic from various points of views

Right Brain Strategies

- Use more stimuli
- Play music
- Sing or play musical instruments
- Use dim lights
- Encourage peer interaction

- Provide enough space for group activities
- Arrange desks in clusters
- Give a lot of group work
- Play social games
- Allow the child to solve a problem by considering problems holistically
- Have brainstorming sessions
- Give tasks that encourage creativity and self-expression
- Invent or re-invent something
- Give open-ended activities
- Provide plenty of hands-on and kinaesthetic tasks
- Use tangible learning tools that the child can interact with
- When teaching math, give real-life examples or use tools
- Teach the child how to read by showing visuals and examples
- When reading, expect that the child will be good in getting the main idea and comprehending the big picture but may have trouble with details. Encourage them to take down notes and make outlines so they can organize important information.
- Write down the main points
- Give study guides
- Emphasize important details
- Illustrate concepts
- Make them create visuals, collages, dioramas, and mobiles.
- Offer opportunities for the child to work with colours, graphics and designs
- Create artworks
- Give tasks that involve awareness of sensations
- Teach with manipulatives
- Have activities dealing with spatial relationships
- Be in touch with emotions
- Make them learn more by doing and experiencing things
- Participate with the subject rather than simply observing from a distance or reading about it
- Discuss philosophy
- Build something without following instructions
- Consider body language when teaching
- Practice skills
- Have role playing and theatre activities
- Make the subject familiar; relate it to something the child already knows

Balancing a Right Brain Dominance

- Teach the child how to organize his/her things and manage time
- Expect that the child will use estimates; help him/her with being more precise if needed
- Make them remember details by teaching mnemonics and other memory techniques
- The child may rely on intuition; teach how to determine when it is appropriate and when it is not
- Help the child organize his/her thoughts

These are just some of the ways that you could suit learning to a child's hemispheric dominance. The following chapter will give you additional advice on how to develop different kinds of intelligence.

Chapter 7. Beyond Left and Right: Developing the Multiple Intelligences

Howard Gardner developed the theory of multiple intelligences. This theory states that people are able to know the world through language, music, mathematical and logical analysis, visual and spatial representations, using the body to create things or solve problems, understanding ourselves, and understanding others. This means that each person has distinct types of intelligences, which can be developed through several ways.

Verbal Skills (Left Brain)

- Encourage him/her to be active in a group
- Let him/her speak his/her mind
- Enrol him/her in creative writing classes
- Suggest that he/she write poems, song lyrics, stories, essays, letters, etc.
- Make the child join writing contests
- Give him/her a diary
- Encourage him/her to learn a new language

Musical Skills (Right Brain)

- Sing and play music together
- Go to music classes with your child
- Let him/her learn how to play a musical instrument or sing
- Let him/her join a choir or singing contest

Logical/Math Skills (Left Brain)

- Give fun puzzles for solving
- Solve math problems together
- Train your child with mental arithmetic skills and speed math
- Discuss issues rationally
- Teach logic and critical thinking skills

Visual/Spatial Skills (Right Brain):

- Draw, color, paint, etc.
- Attend art and design classes
- Teach how to read different kinds of maps
- Make the child plot his/her route to destinations

- Make him/her learn how to use a compass to navigate around
- Let the child walk around a safe environment with a blindfold on

Bodily Movement Skills (Right Brain)

- Let the child participate in sports
- Dance as he/she pleases
- Exercise
- Play active games
- Build things

Intrapersonal Skills (Right Brain)

- Discuss self-help methods
- Know how to manage emotions and teach the techniques to your child
- Let him/her reflect on his/her experiences and actions
- Encourage the child to think about why he/she does things

Interpersonal Skills (Left Brain)

- Make the child interact with different kinds of people (but make sure that they won't harm the child!)
- Brainstorm about why somebody is acting a certain way
- Teach about being unbiased and unprejudiced
- Let the child consider how his/her actions or words might affect somebody else

Learn more about the multiple intelligences so you could enhance your child's overall talents. An Indigo will do his/her tasks better and live a more fulfilling life if you took a holistic approach to his/her growth.

Chapter 8. Evaluating Hemispheric Dominance Strategies: The Pros and Cons of Brain Based Learning

Although brain based learning has several advantages, it's not perfect. Here are the pros and cons so you know what to expect from it.

Pros

Tackles Learning More Deeply

Brain based learning led to a greater focus on brain function as a whole. This led people to look into other aspects of intelligence such as meta-cognition, executive functioning, multiple intelligences, and the like.

Deals with Classroom-Relevant Concerns

Brain-based learning deals with sensory perceptions, attention, memory, and emotions. It gives techniques to gain and keep attention of students.

Customized Lesson Plans

The child learns better and faster because teaching strategies are suited to his/her learning styles. Assessments can also be adjusted to measure the child's progress more accurately.

Monitoring of Progress

Knowing how the left and right brains function allows people to monitor their performance in a child. By monitoring progress, it's possible to improve their functions. A student's progress is not measured by tests alone but also through his/her demonstrations, writings, and creations.

Uses New Techniques

Traditional teaching techniques have their limitation, which brain-based teaching styles are making up for. The student also has the opportunity to learn more.

More Holistic Engagement

The child is seen to be more than a sponge of information but an individual who has unique characteristics that cause him/her to respond differently to various teaching approaches. When people consider the child's hemisphere dominance, they will understand him/her more and interact with him/her more appropriately. This allows the child to be more engaged in the subject or task.

Supports Creativity, Flexibility, and Individuality

Dealing with brain-based learning techniques makes teachers and caregivers find other means of teaching the child. It also enhances the child's creativity and individual expression. Since free self-expression is important in building identity, it ultimately encourages the child to be comfortable with who he/she is.

Reduces Stress

Traditional classroom settings may be stressful for a child if it doesn't suit his/her preferences. Music, soft lighting, and other factors can be used to produce calming atmospheres.

Encourages Bonding

In the teachers and caregivers' quest to fit the material to the child's characteristics, they will know the child more and will bond to him/her better. This is especially important for the emotionally sensitive indigos.

Respects the Child

The child has a say over how he/she will learn. This encourages responsibility and cooperation and boosts the child's self-esteem. Children can also teach and learn from one another, enhancing their learning abilities, socialization skills, and expressiveness. They take a more active role in their learning thus they learn better.

Better Problem Solving

Methods of problem solving are now not limited to what the teacher instructs, but the students may solve it in their own ways. This is important because they can learn how to come up with solutions without having to be told how it's done, thus fostering independence and resourcefulness.

Includes Practical Simulations and Experiences

The child will learn how to apply the information through simulations and experiential learning. The learning acquired from these can be transferred to a wide variety of disciplines. The immersion will benefit right brainers since they learn better from experience and retain information much longer. This also sends a message to the child that it's okay to commit mistakes and he/she can learn a lot from them. The hands on-activities encourage team work and gives opportunities for students to take care of their learning process.\

Cons

New Field

Brain-based learning is still in the early stages so more studies and trials need to be done before it is accepted in the mainstream.

Not Much Support from Experts

Not many experts support this kind of teaching since there is not much evidence to back it up.

Lack of Experimental Data

Compared to other teaching techniques, brain based learning hasn't undergone much testing yet. Thus, some people label it as pseudo-scientific.

Can Encourage Stereotyping

Labeling a person as a left-brainer or a right-brainer can cause people to have prejudices of him/her.

Can Be Expensive

Brain based learning requires special resources, media and professional expertise which are not feely available. This increases costs.

More Challenging

Students may not be used to exerting extra efforts in school. Brain based learning requires more focus on students, which requires an increased number of staff.

Consider the pros and cons of brain-based learning before committing to a teaching program. Learn more about it so you could do some of the techniques on your own. This will help you save costs.

Chapter 9. Raising an Indigo Child: Some Tips and Warnings

The previous chapters dealt mostly with the intellectual development of an Indigo child. Here are some more tried and tested tips to raise an Indigo well.

Encourage Creativity and Expression

Indigos are energetic souls. Allow them to speak their minds and to create whatever they want, but be there for them as a guide and protector. Create a safe space in the home where they can vent when they need to. Channel an Indigo's abundant energy through physical activities, creative pursuits, and safe explorations.

Listen Deeply

Do not focus only on the words they are using, but try to read between the lines. Because they are mostly right brain dominant, they may not express themselves well verbally. There will be times when they say things that do not really represent what they are feeling. Connect with them on an emotional level instead. Do not be distracted with their language but figure out what they really want. Help them put their thoughts and emotions into words. Be patient with them when they're being difficult to understand.

Mind Your Body Language

They are more attuned to how things are being said than most people. This means that they will hear more than what you say. Try to mean what you are saying because they will know when you are lying. Make sure that your non-verbal expression supports your verbal message. Make eye contact. Use appropriate gestures and tone of voice so they will understand what you're saying more clearly. Study my book on NLP.

Socialize Them

Indigo children need to interact with others so they will become emotionally stable and socially competent individuals. You can start first with people who are easy to be with, such as family, caregivers, other Indigo children and people with positive vibes. Gradually introduce them to different kinds of folks (but of course, not to the dangerous type). They were sent with a mission. Respect and amplify that. You will not know the mission until much later.

Live a Healthy Lifestyle

Indigos can be sensitive to the environment and to food. If you could, live in a place where there is fresh air and lots of sunlight. Visit nature regularly as this is very energizing for them. Stay away from unhealthy food and eat healthy, organic ones. Avoid smoking and drinking so that your child will not copy you. Make your child exercise regularly to keep the body fit and the mind sharp. These substances may dull their mind and mess up their sensitive vibrations. Watch out for allergens as Indigos are sensitive to them. You can train the child to take care of him or herself even at a young age. Indigos are naturally independent. Fasting and affirmations are a nice addition to usual routines.

Meditate

Meditation has a lot of positive effects for both mind and body. Learn more about meditation and encourage your child to meditate regularly. Doing so may also help him/her become more attuned to his/her purpose. Getting to know the auras and chakras is important. Mindfulness and selfness are also part of the general picture of an indigo child.

Connect With the Child

Know what's happening to him/her, however do not be too nosey because they might clam up. Allow them to open up to you when they are comfortable. If you can't do that, find someone or something that will help him/her to loosen up. Spend a lot of time together and regularly talk with one another.

Brain Training

Indigo children are typically smarter than average. Consider brain training your child. You can find a lot of brain training materials online. Make your home stimulating by acquiring a variety of books and learning materials. Look at my other books on NLP, EFT, memorization techniques, speed reading etc... They were all written for this aim and for my son.

TV and Your Indigo Child

Since many shows are not really good for children, it's best not to let them watch TV. Staying away from television can add more time for learning about the world and interacting with other people. However, you can also encourage the child to watch shows that contribute to his/her intellectual and emotional development, or at least are pleasant to watch. I encouraged my son to watch the world about us, tomorrow's world, David Attenborough's films, Jean Jacque Cousteau's series etc...

Discipline

Indigo children have their own ideas of what is right and wrong, so you need to teach them what is acceptable behavior and what is not. Teach them how to manage their emotions and to consider the effects of their behavior - this will make them less impulsive and more successful in life later on.

Do not punish them though with verbal or physical abuse - traditional ways of discipline do not work with them. Instead, set clear rules and consequences for not adhering to them. Uphold them consistently; if you don't, you will teach the child that the rules are arbitrary and can be broken sometimes.

Punishing is counter-productive since it creates negative feelings, which decreases a child's capability to think. Instead, reward good behaviors and ignore bad ones. If you must punish, consider giving time outs. Make the child think about what he or she has done for a few minutes. Talk with the child afterwards.

Punishing is a form of giving attention, which is rewarding – and when something is rewarded, it tends to be repeated. Try to hold your temper whenever the child is acting out; if you lash out, you will just teach him/her that violence solves problems and he/she will also become violent when he/she grows up.

Discuss why you are imposing the rules. Indigos need to know the whys before complying with something. They will not respond to being forced. You may also ask the child's help in setting the rules. This way, they can follow the rules more.

Teaching Responsibility

Free-spirited Indigos need to learn how to be responsible. Discuss the importance of being responsible and demonstrate responsibility yourself – these kids learn more from example and not through preaching. Make the child think about the positive results of accomplishing the task and the negative consequences of avoiding it.

You can turn chores and duties into games, but expect that the child might consider it as a form of manipulation. You may say that you are doing that to make the task easier, not necessarily to trick him/her into doing it. Discuss how you can commit to responsibilities better. This will train him/her to become a responsible adult.

Give Respect

An Indigo is an old and advanced soul. Do not think that just because an Indigo is child, he/she is stupid and can be treated as such. Showing respect will teach him/her to respect others, which is important since Indigos tend to act like royalty (since they are royalty in the spiritual sense). This does not mean being a pushover though. Respecting includes disciplining them whenever necessary, but do this out of a genuine desire to teach respect and not to exert control over him/her. My son had his fair share of these teaching disciplines.

Maintain a Pleasant Environment

Create a relaxing atmosphere in the home. Indigos are sensitive to stress. Observe the child to see what soothes him/her. You can also ask what you could do to make the house better. We got interested in Fen-shui because of him.

Be considerate of the child's feelings. Indigos are more sensitive to emotions because of their high frequency vibrations. If you get into a fight with somebody, try not to do it where your child will see you.

Consider all your kids as valuable whether they are Indigos or not. Kids are sensitive to favoritism and they will fight one another if not equally cared for. Avoid making them compete for your attention even if it makes you feel wanted. Be a loving parent to all of them so they will get along well and grow up to be self-assured individuals. I only had one child so I did not have the problem.

Find activities that you can do with your children so you can bond with all of them, but avoid those that involve competing against one another. Also, whenever there is conflict within the home, seek to resolve it as soon as possible. Talk with them so you can find ways to solve problems together. This will keep your family intact even through tough times. The indigo child will shine in any case.

Nurture Spirituality

Indigos are highly spiritual even when young. Explore spiritual concepts with your child. Do not force him/her to accept your own religion though – let him/her decide what spiritual path to take. Listen to him/her – you might learn something new since Indigos are spiritual teachers too.

Indigo Children and ADHD

Indigo children are often diagnosed with ADHD. Be informed that having ADHD does not automatically mean that your child must take ADHD medication. If your doctor prescribes them, get a second opinion. It can be managed without having to resort to dangerous drugs.

Although ADHD is considered as a disability, some see it as an evolutionary advantage. According to some researchers, our ancient ancestors with ADHD may have had higher chances of survival and were valuable members of their tribe. Because they had restless minds and abundant energy, they hunted more, were more vigilant against dangers, and reproduced more. This theory was confirmed by recent studies of a nomadic tribe.

In the present time, ADHD creates an unrestrained mind, dissatisfaction with the status quo, and a passion for action. These are characteristics that bring about radical change. So, if your child is diagnosed with ADHD, you can consider it as a blessing. What you can do is learn more about it, help your child cope with it and make the most out of it.

Needs of an Indigo Child

To raise a happy Indigo child, know what his/her dreams are. It's possible that he/she is yearning for the following:

- The world becomes a better place to live in
- There are no poor people
- Money is not a problem
- Consumers are not tricked into buying what they don't really need
- Resources are abundant
- People don't hog wealth and resources for themselves
- People are living healthy lifestyles
- Dangerous substances are no longer used for food and drinks
- Nature is taken care of
- Pollution is eradicated
- The ill and disabled are taken care of
- Children will have greater choice over what and how they would learn
- People will have more freedom over the life they will live
- Families will be more loving towards one another
- Each individual is part of a supportive community
- Political systems are not corrupt
- Governance is for the greater good of the people
- No wars and in-fighting
- Every human cooperates with one another to better the entire planet
- People are no longer praised for being competitive and taking advantage of others
- Respect is given to all
- Everyone is treated equally regardless of what their race, sex, or religion is
- No one is manipulating another person for the sake of selfish purposes
- Everyone is striving for personal and collective growth
- Education is for all
- There is no more dumbing down of the society anymore
- News reflect unbiased views
- Beneficial information is not kept secret
- Education does not focus only on getting a job but also in making meaningful contributions to society
- People are taught what really matters in life such as self-sufficiency, emotional intelligence, character building, responsibility, empathy, etc.

An indigo child may have lofty goals. Try to support them instead of saying how impossible or difficult they are to achieve. Help him/her find ways to translate their hopes into realities. Find other people who are working towards the same goals. The time is ripe for good changes to happen; you and your child only have to push things a bit. You can only gain.

Conclusion

Thank you again for downloading this book!

I hope this book was able to help you understand Indigo children, their hemispheric dominance, and how to take care of them well.

Indigos are wonderful beings that need your love and care. Even if they become difficult at times, remember that they are like that because they have an important mission to fulfill. Do your part in helping the world progress by being the best parent or caregiver that you can be. Good luck in your exciting adventure! I was in it. Now is your turn.

About the author

Paul has studied Electronic Medicine. Electronic Medicine is a set of modalities and tools that enable the body to be rebalanced, reset. Balancing the meridians does this. He is also a Reiki Master in Usui and Seichim and has been for many years. He is a qi-gong practitioner and practices every day. He composes music and write songs. In his twenties, he was a psychologist in France where he also studied neuromusicology. He holds a Honors degree from a British University and prepared a Doctorate of Philosophy in metaphysical sciences. He studied acupuncture with the Beijing college of Acupuncture and practices auriculo-therapy on a daily basis. He shares his time between Europe and Latin America. His healing sessions are always free.

All of his books started with a personal life experience. His best teacher and mentor, as he says, is the University of Life. "Nothing beats the understanding depth that it brings", he explains while adding the old adage: "when the student is ready, the teacher comes".

Other books by the author

.

AWAKEN Series:

AWAKEN Your Auras – Series I – Book One

AWAKEN Your Chakras – Series I – Book Two

AWAKEN Your Third Eye – Series I – Book Three

AWAKEN Your Mind – Series I – Book Four

AWAKEN Your Self – Series I – Book Five

AWAKEN Your Knowledge – Series I – Book Six

Power Healing New Series –

Power Healing: EFT – Series II – Volume One

Power Healing: NLP – Series II – Volume Two

Power Healing: I–Ching and DNA – Series II – Volume Three

Power Thinking Series

Power Thinking: The Efficient Mind (Hemispheric dominance, Speed reading and Memorization techniques), Accelerated Learning

Power Playing – Series III –

- Ancient Magic Stone

Predictoscope™